Practical
CLIMBING
PLANTS

Patrick Johns

The Crowood Press

First published in 1994 by
The Crowood Press Ltd
Ramsbury, Marlborough
Wiltshire SN8 2HR

British Library Cataloguing-in-Publication Data

A catalogue record for this book is available from the British
Library.

ISBN 1 85223 777 5

Picture Credits
All photographs by Patrick Johns
Line-drawings by Claire Upsdale-Jones

Typeset in Optima by Chippendale Type Ltd,
Otley, West Yorkshire
Printed and bound by Paramount Printing Group, Hong Kong

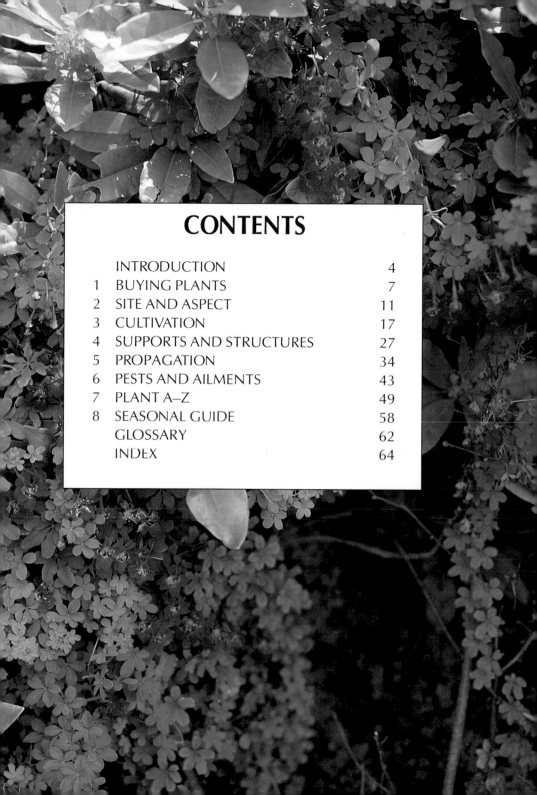

CONTENTS

INTRODUCTION

The majority of gardens have a boundary fence or wall; in any case, the dwelling has at least one wall suitable for supporting plants. These structures provide shelter and protection for plants, at the same time making them look more attractive; a dreary fence can be made to look much brighter when it is furnished with an interesting plant. Structures like sheds, garages and outhouses all provide suitable surfaces to adorn with plants. In some cases, plants provide welcome camouflage when the structure has seen better days!

Climbers and wall plants add another dimension to gardening. Some plants, that might not otherwise survive in a locality, will flourish when introduced to the added warmth and shelter that a wall or similar structure can provide; a south-facing wall is especially good for the more tender plants. While a cottage in the country with roses trained around the door is not within reach of some people, there is no reason why an attractive feature could not be constructed in any garden. A simple wigwam constructed with bamboo canes could make a focal point, as could a pergola or arch, and there are many other interesting features that could be made by a DIY enthusiast. A visit to most garden centres will provide food for thought.

Although true climbing plants — those able to support themselves by various means — like ivy are often grown, the range can easily be extended by the provision of a simple support for those like clematis, climbing roses, and fan-trained specimens like peach trees and others, which need a

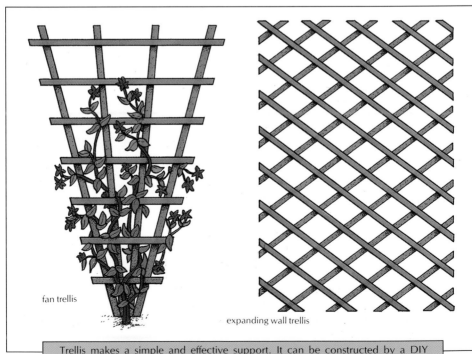

fan trellis

expanding wall trellis

Trellis makes a simple and effective support. It can be constructed by a DIY enthusiast or purchased ready made.

If possible, tree stumps should be removed to prevent armillaria *disease from becoming established in the garden. Alternatively, some people make an attractive feature out of them.*

*Winter-flowering Jasmine (*Jasminum nudiflorum) *blossom is much appreciated during the dark winter months.*

little assistance. Free-standing plants like certain viburnums can also be very effective when grown alongside a wall. Some annual plants like sweet peas are useful, since they can furnish an area before permanent planting takes place, perhaps when redesigning

Take care to select a plant that is suited to its support; a heavy plant would soon topple light framework.

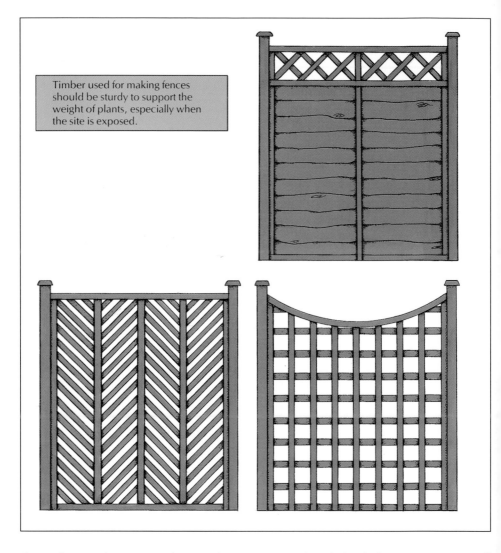

Timber used for making fences should be sturdy to support the weight of plants, especially when the site is exposed.

the garden, or when you need to spend time thinking over more elaborate plans after moving into a new property.

Some plants are very vigorous and so consideration should be given to what consequences there may be in planting any particular kind. For example, wisteria is a very attractive climber but it is notorious for creeping under roof tiles; thick stems expanding behind down-pipes may pull them from the wall, and the roots of certain plants have a tendency to enter drains and may damage foundations below ground. However, there is no reason why any of these problems should arise if sufficient care is taken in selection, and in most situations, proper maintenance of the plant.

1 • BUYING PLANTS

It is easy to buy a plant, but to obtain a good plant for the correct situation takes a little thought and consideration.

Market stalls sometimes have bargains for sale; other sources include garden centres, open days at gardens open to the general public, superstores, high-street shops, friends and neighbours. A great number of plants are purchased on impulse, despite the amount of advice against doing this. Plant labels are now generally very informative and it is worth doing a little research on the plant before purchase: a wise choice will give pleasure for many years to come.

The type of questions that need to be answered include those concerning soil type. Does the plant need an acid, or alkaline growing medium? Moisture regime is important: will it tolerate prolonged dryness at the root? Some plants will make shoot growth in moderately dry soil, but if the roots are too dry during mid-summer when the plant should be initiating flower buds for next spring – a distinct possibility

Wisteria sinensis Chinese wisteria
Hardiness: Hardy.
Care rating: Easy.
Description: Deciduous twiner with woody stems.
Peak interest: Summer.
Growth rate: Fast.
Soil needs: Fertile and well drained.
Treatment: Cut back current season's growth to five leaves in summer, then to three buds in winter.
Propagation: By bench grafting in winter; by seed in autumn or spring.

Abeliophyllum distichum *produces its delicate flowers before the foliage.*

when growing close to a wall – the display may be disappointing. Shade tolerance is another point to bear in mind since some subjects will only give of their best in full sun. Hardiness is also very important, especially in northern gardens.

Some plants are toxic in one way or another and so if pets or young children are likely to come into contact with them, make sure the berries, leaves or sap will not cause harm. The health of the plant itself is important and any sign of pests, diseases or other problems means that it is worth looking for a better specimen; there is usually a good selection unless the plant is rare in cultivation.

*Ivy (*Hedera helix*) is a good plant for ground cover, or to clad a wall.*

Virtually all climbers, and the majority of wall plants, are sold in containers. Container-grown plants should be well established in the container. They are usually more expensive than 'bare-root' plants lifted from the field. The main advantage of the container-grown plant is that it can be planted at any time of the year. Bare-root plants that are containerized and offered for sale immediately are no better than ordinary bare-root specimens, except that they may have suitable material around the roots to add to the soil at planting time. The rootball of a plant should adhere to the container when it is picked up by the stem.

Warning Signs

Before buying a plant, check that it is not suffering from any of the following:

1. Surface moss, lichen or weeds on growing medium.
2. Roots growing out of top or bottom of container.
3. Drooping leaves with parched container contents.
4. Abnormal spindly or straggly growth. (Trained specimens should be of good shape – that is what the extra cost is for!)
5. Starved, weak stems, with lower leaves missing or yellow when they should be green.
6. Drooping leaves with wet soil suggests a root disorder.
7. Broken stems and branches.
8. In variegated plants, reverted, green shoots (although these can usually be satisfactorily cut out).
9. Soft growth caused by forcing.
10. Tender plants stood out for display without protection.

Roots growing out of the drainage holes in the base of a container suggest neglect and starvation.

Cost

Some plants do look rather expensive at first, but if a specimen is healthy, it is worth considering that it will give pleasure for very many years, so it is really a very good investment. Plants that are being sold unusually cheaply should be examined closely; it is usually safer to buy from a reliable source and pay a bit extra.

Clematis x 'Nelly Moser' trained on a tripod makes an attractive feature.

Clematis x 'Nelly Moser'
Hardiness: Hardy.
Care rating: Easy.
Description: A vigorous deciduous plant.
Peak interest: Spring and summer.
Growth rate: Fast.
Soil needs: Well-drained loam.
Treatment: Keep roots cool. Cut back congested growth in winter to within 3ft (1m) of the ground.
Propagation: By layering in spring, or by half-ripe cuttings in summer.

Transport

Take care to avoid chilling the plant on the journey home. This may not be such an important factor with leafless deciduous plants, but evergreens can be severely checked in an open-backed lorry, or on the roof of a car. A plastic bin liner will help to protect the plant if that really is the only means of transport.

Once you get the plant home, ensure that it is safely protected from strong wind:

If planting cannot take place immediately, one method of protecting the roots from drying out is to heel them into a shallow trench and cover them with soil. The plants should be placed at an angle to protect them from damage by wind.

Cytisus battandieri
Hardiness: Hardy, except in very cold areas.
Care rating: Easy.
Description: Deciduous, vigorous, silvery-leaved shrub.
Peak interest: Late spring to early summer.
Growth rate: Fairly fast.
Soil needs: Well-drained loam.
Treatment: Transplant container-raised plants; bare-root plants are difficult to establish.
Propagation: By seed.

plants in containers are easily blown over unless they are supported. Bare-root plants are also at risk and a further precaution should be taken to prevent the roots from drying out before planting. Cover the roots with soil or damp sacking; better still, dig a shallow trench, insert the roots so that the plant is at an angle to prevent wind rock, then cover the roots.

Plants on occasion are wrapped in straw or some other material for despatch. In addition to conserving moisture, the plant will be protected from frost and mechanical damage. The material should be removed as soon as possible otherwise fungal diseases may be encouraged to attack the plant.

Roots sometimes dry out in transit. They can usually be revived by soaking them in a container of water. However, that should be avoided when possible and only used as a last resort.

2 • SITE AND ASPECT

Different gardens, even in the same locality, can differ from each other. For example, soil type is inclined to vary dramatically in some areas, from acid sand to alkaline loam; other things being equal, mature gardens with overshadowing trees that restrict the entry of sunlight are likely to benefit some plants, yet be detrimental to others. It is, therefore, not always advisable to select plants that generally perform well in the local neighbourhood, although the area could provide some useful suggestions.

Walls and other structures certainly provide shelter but they can also cause problems. Frost pockets can be created by solid barriers when the barrier is situated at the base of a slope. This is because cold air is heavier than warm air, and so it rolls down and collects at the base. Wind hitting a solid barrier rides over the top and then the

Lathyrus grandiflorus Everlasting pea
Hardiness: Hardy.
Care rating: Easy.
Description: Tendril climber with soft stems.
Peak interest: Summer.
Growth rate: Fast.
Soil needs: Well-drained and fertile.
Treatment: Cut down to ground level in late autumn.
Propagation: By seed.

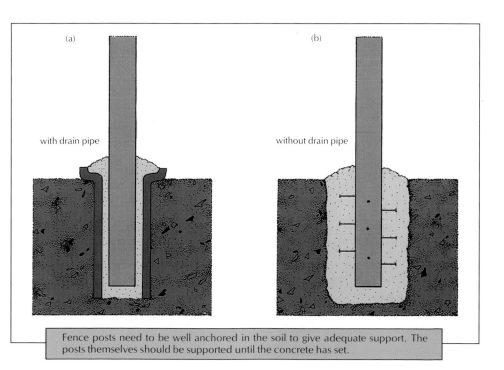

(a)

with drain pipe

(b)

without drain pipe

Fence posts need to be well anchored in the soil to give adequate support. The posts themselves should be supported until the concrete has set.

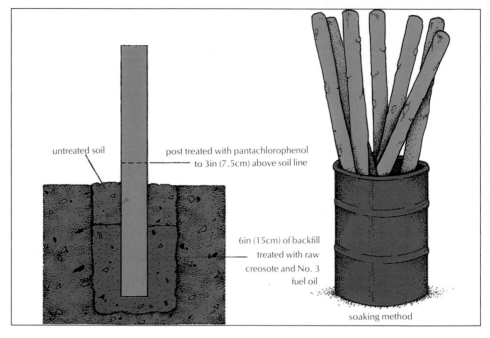

untreated soil

post treated with pantachlorophenol to 3in (7.5cm) above soil line

6in (15cm) of backfill treated with raw creosote and No. 3 fuel oil

soaking method

Well-preserved posts should last for many years.

Jasminum polyanthum has fragrant blossom.

blast makes contact with the ground on the other side with some force. Eddies of cold, draughty air can be created by solid structures. On the other hand, a wall or fence can provide good protection, enabling certain plants to grow in a location that would otherwise be too cold for them to survive.

A southerly aspect, or one facing west is normally warmer than one facing east or north. Since a site facing south enjoys sunlight for more hours of the day (especially in winter) including the sun at midday, it is the warmest of all. An easterly aspect gains the benefit of early morning sun but that, in winter and early spring at least, coincides with air still chilled by a cold night, so it takes longer to warm up, by which time the sun may have moved on. A westerly aspect can also be limited in the amount of direct sunlight it receives, although it can be very useful for those subjects that flower in early spring. Select hardy plants for the north-facing aspect: it is usually the coldest with the least amount of sun. There is a wide range of plants available and so even the coldest of gardens need not be without year-round interest.

Containers

While the majority of climbers and wall shrubs will be planted permanently in the ground, containers come into their own when they are placed on a dwarf wall or, for example, alongside a pergola.

An inexpensive project can be created by growing annual plants from seed and allowing them to climb up a support. A container such as the one illustrated could even be made from a plastic bucket!

Lonicera periclymenum   Honeysuckle, Woodbine
Hardiness: Hardy.
Care rating: Easy.
Description: Twining deciduous climber with fragrant flowers.
Peak interest: Summer.
Growth rate: Fast.
Soil needs: Fertile and well-drained.
Treatment: Cut out flowered wood after flowers fade.
Propagation: By seed in spring, or by cuttings in summer or late autumn.

One advantage to growing plants in containers is that they can be moved around; tender subjects can even be taken into more favourable conditions during winter. Another is that they provide the opportunity to give prominence to specimens with a definite seasonal interest, so that they can be replaced by others as necessary. Containers are also invaluable when the ground is unsuitable for direct planting – on a patio or courtyard, for instance. Sunken containers filled with appropriate rooting medium facilitate the growing of permanent

Long bamboo canes tied at the top to form a wig-wam make an excellent support for climbing plants.

Wooden containers should be treated with preservative, and proprietary compounds are available for the purpose. The compressed peat containers have a limited life of approximately one year.

Plant containers should always be supported slightly above the ground to assist drainage. This should prevent the roots from becoming waterlogged, prevent worms from entering the container, and help to avoid damage to the container in frosty weather.

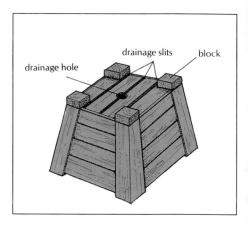

It is important to ensure that containers permit sufficient drainage. Raising the container off the ground will help.

plants that would otherwise be unhappy in the existing soil; they will also restrict the roots of an over-vigorous subject, thus allowing more controlled growth.

Containers are available in a wide range of materials, including terracotta, plastic, wood, concrete, fibreglass and compressed peat. Imported terracotta is sometimes subject to flaking during frosty weather and so should be protected. This material, together with concrete products, needs to be soaked before use so that salts are removed; if this isn't done, the salts will diffuse to the outside of the container and look unsightly.

When selecting a container, it is important to consider the likely future of the plant. For instance, if the plant is likely to need moving into a larger container at some later date, select one with straight sides so that the rootball will slip out without damage. Another point to remember is that plant diseases may be present in a previously used container and so it is advisable to wash it out thoroughly before use. In any case, the interior needs to be clean and dry so that the roots do not cling to the sides making them difficult to remove.

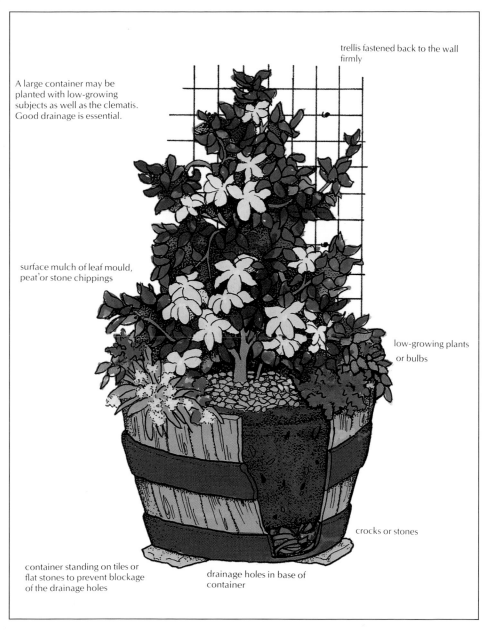

trellis fastened back to the wall firmly

A large container may be planted with low-growing subjects as well as the clematis. Good drainage is essential.

surface mulch of leaf mould, peat'or stone chippings

low-growing plants or bulbs

crocks or stones

container standing on tiles or flat stones to prevent blockage of the drainage holes

drainage holes in base of container

Proper drainage must be provided for plants growing in a container. This will help to keep the roots healthy and also prevent the container from bursting with frost in winter.

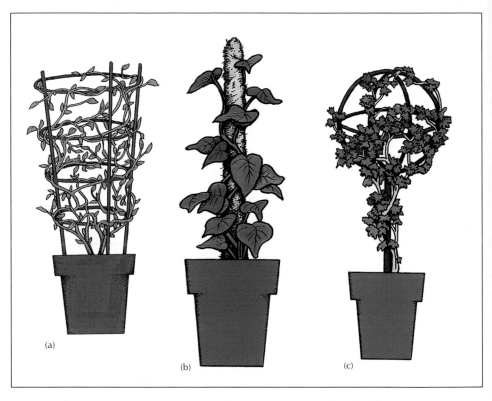

(a)

(b)

(c)

Vigorous plants soon outgrow their support unless growth is adapted. The plant illustrated (a) has been trained into a spiral. A moss pole (b) is a perfect support for climbers with aerial roots. Metal frames (c) can be made into any number of different shapes and used as supports for small-leaved climbers.

The kind of planting medium (often incorrectly called 'compost') needs to be given consideration. Some plants will not tolerate an alkaline medium; others do not thrive when conditions are too acid. The most suitable medium for the majority of shrubs is a mixture of loam, peat, sand and fertilizer; lime is also necessary for most subjects. Loamless medium in various compounds can be obtained from garden centres and other retailers, but it is more difficult to maintain because it tends to dry out faster

and long-term container subjects are inclined to become starved of certain minor elements over a period of time.

To facilitate watering, sufficient space should be left between the rim of the container and the surface of the rootball. It is very important to ensure the complete root is moistened at each application, otherwise roots will be encouraged to grow only at the surface. It is also important to ensure that the rootball is moist in its existing container before it is transferred into the new one.

3 • CULTIVATION

Planting

Once planted, a perennial subject is likely to be in the same position for many years and so the ground should be well prepared. In addition to digging over the top few inches, it is advisable to dig down into the subsoil of the second 'spit'. Sometimes a hard layer of soil or mineral matter is present, which impedes drainage during winter and is likely to obstruct the passage of subsoil moisture, preventing it from reaching the plants in summer. This 'pan' is usually easily removed by using a digging fork, although on occasions a crowbar is necessary. In addition to removing weeds, debris, and possibly improving drainage, another purpose of digging is to incorporate rotted manure, garden compost, leaf mould, or some other form of bulky organic material to help improve soil fertility. Digging, provided it is carried out at the right time, also helps to improve crumb structure and tilth. Heavy clay should be dug in autumn when

Rosa x 'Cecile Brunner' Climbing rose
Hardiness: Hardy.
Care rating: Easy.
Description: Climbing plant with stiff prickly stems.
Peak interest: Summer.
Growth rate: Fast.
Soil needs: Fertile and moist but well-drained.
Treatment: Remove dead wood in winter; deadhead spent flowers.
Propagation: By budding in summer, or by hardwood cuttings in late autumn.

Archways are simple structures to erect. They can be made from tubular steel, although timber and brick is usually more attractive until plants cover the feature.

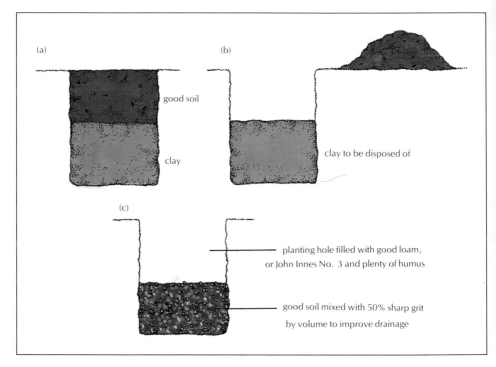

(a)

good soil

clay

(b)

clay to be disposed of

(c)

planting hole filled with good loam,
or John Innes No. 3 and plenty of humus

good soil mixed with 50% sharp grit
by volume to improve drainage

A cold, wet clay soil can be made more congenial by removing the second 'spit', then filling the hole with good soil. Alternatively, mix grit with the subsoil and top up the hole with good soil or John Innes No. 3.

the soil is still comparatively dry. Left rough, the winter frost will shatter the clods so that they can be raked fine in late spring. Sandy soil should be left until spring before digging, otherwise winter rain will probably cause the surface to pan.

Certain plants will thrive only in acid soil, while others require alkaline conditions; fortunately, there is a good selection that is not too particular, but the nutrient status and pH level of the soil should be determined before planting. Simple kits for testing the soil are available from garden centres and other retail establishments. Full instructions for use will be found in the kit, together with the amount of lime necessary to bring the soil to the correct pH level for the plants

in question. Similar testing kits are available for assessing whether fertilizers are necessary. Lime is best applied a few weeks before planting so that it has a chance to work on the soil in good time.

Unless the ground needs to be cultivated for some other reason, it should not really be necessary to cultivate much more than the root area that the new plant is going to take up initially. However, it is important to dig out a hole sufficiently large to accommodate the roots without buckling. The best way to see how large a hole is required is to place the plant on the ground and trace round the root system, allowing extra space so that the base of the hole can be forked over easily. The hole should be dug to such

Rambling roses and other climbing plants make good companions for an established tree. Set the climber a short distance away from the tree trunk and keep it well watered during the first summer.

Clematis rhederiana *provides a bonus with bell-shaped flowers and attractive seed heads.*

helps to move bare-root plants up and down slightly, but this should be done carefully. Firm planting is important and is best done by treading the soil firmly around the roots, taking care not to damage the roots or stem. Check that the plant is at the

Robinia hispida *has brittle stems and is best grown against a wall.*

a depth that when the plant is inserted, the soil mark on the stem is level with the final soil surface. In the case of a containerized plant, the top of the rootball should be level with the final soil surface. A forkful of bulky organic material worked into the base of the hole will help to create the right conditions for the plant's establishment, but avoid placing a wad of the material in the hole because it may act as a sump and waterlog the roots.

If there is any delay in planting when there is a strong, cold wind blowing, cover the roots of bare-root plants with sacking or polythene; better still, leave them heeled in until the last minute. Once the plant has been placed centrally in the hole, trickle soil in around the roots; when doing this, it

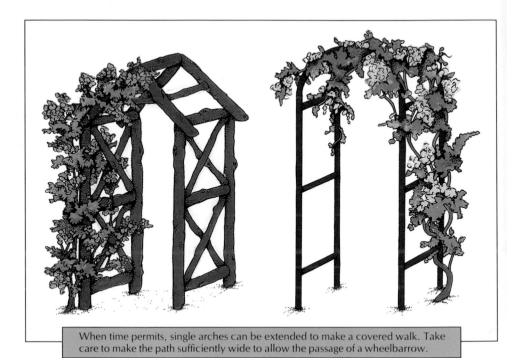

When time permits, single arches can be extended to make a covered walk. Take care to make the path sufficiently wide to allow the passage of a wheelbarrow.

correct depth, then rake over the soil surface to finish off. All that remains is to ensure that the soil is moist by watering if necessary, and then to tie the plant to its support. A surface mulch of bulky organic matter will help to conserve moisture during the following summer.

Plants raised in containers can be planted at any time of the year provided the soil is not too wet or frozen. Do ensure that the rootball itself is moist before taking it out of the container, otherwise the roots may not take up water once the ball is in the ground. Bare-root plants, however, are likely to receive too much of a check when they are planted at the wrong time. Aim to get evergreens planted during autumn when the soil is still reasonably warm; failing that, plant them in spring. The best time to plant bare-root deciduous plants is during the dormant season after leaf fall; any time

between late autumn and early spring is desirable, although autumn is preferable.

Evergreens are likely to lose some if not all of their leaves during the first winter after planting. It is the plant's safeguard against excessive moisture loss through transpiration. Large evergreen shrubs often benefit from having their stems cut back by half at planting time. This helps to reduce the strain on roots.

Watering

When you consider that over ninety per cent of a plant is made up of moisture, it is easy to see how important it is to keep the plant supplied with that commodity. Water is important in other ways: it is the medium via which nutrients are taken up through the roots from the soil; it moves food around

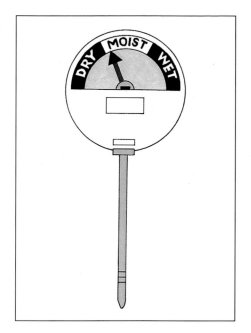

A simple moisture meter will indicate when watering is necessary.

and possibly too wet; if the soil binds together without releasing a visible amount of moisture, then shatters when it is dropped to the ground, it is probably just right. The ideal level to check is at root depth and so a soil auger is a useful tool for taking samples at various depths. This tool resembles a large corkscrew and can be made out of a wood-boring auger.

A surface mulch applied when the soil is moist in spring will help to conserve moisture, prevent leaching of nutrients and suppress annual weed growth.

within the plant; it is an important factor in photosynthesis, the food-manufacturing process within the plant; it keeps the plant turgid, and it also helps to keep it cool when necessary. When the plant is short of water it will suffer stress, and if dryness is prolonged, the plant could die. Conversely, if the soil is too wet and waterlogged, there will be insufficient air to circulate around the roots and the plant will not thrive.

Experienced gardeners will know by the look of the plant and by the feel of the soil whether or not sufficient moisture is present. However, for those who need them, there are various gadgets available to indicate whether irrigation is necessary. Otherwise, the simplest method is to take a handful of soil from close to the root system and squeeze it in the palm of the hand. If water oozes from between the fingers, then the soil is likely to be sufficiently moist –

The first summer after planting is a critical time for the plant and so every effort should be made to ensure the soil is kept moist at that time. When irrigating a plant, it is important to moisten the root system thoroughly, otherwise the roots will tend to grow only at the surface where they are more likely to be prone to drought. The evening is the best time to apply water as it is less likely to be lost through evaporation. Overhead watering by lawn sprinklers and similar devices is convenient but when used during warm, sunny weather much of the water is lost through evaporation. Wastage also occurs when water is applied directly from the open end of a hose, as much of it goes straight to drainage. The ideal

Tropaeolum peregrinum will clamber over a structure with little assistance.

fertilizer is often necessary to top up the reserve. These plant foods are usually very concentrated and so care needs to be taken in their application: do not exceed the recommended dose in the hope that the plant will grow faster, or produce better flowers. Make sure the soil is moist at the time of application; the fertilizer can be lightly raked into the surface, or it could be watered in. Foliar feeding can be carried out, particularly in the case of a sickly plant with poor roots; the dose is very dilute and, generally, it is better to keep fertilizer away from the leaves because they can easily be scorched.

Proprietary compounds made up especially for shrubs and flowers are available. They are easily applied and full instructions for use will be found on the container. Some are applied dry, while others can be dissolved in water for liquid feeding. The latter are useful for plants growing in

watering system uses underground perforated tubes, but this is beyond the scope of most gardeners. A good compromise is to use a rigid or lay-flat polythene tube placed flat on the surface of the soil; one end is closed up, while the other is attached to the water source.

Feeding

Green plants are able to make food in their leaves during daylight hours by the process of photosynthesis, but they rely on their roots to take up certain essential nutrients from the soil. The plant foods need to be replaced from time to time in the form of fertilizer. Farmyard manure and well-made garden compost would provide most of the nutrients necessary to keep the plant healthy, but an annual dressing of general

Akebia x *pentaphylla*   Chocolate vine
Hardiness: Hardy.
Care rating: Easy.
Description: Vigorous deciduous plant.
Peak interest: Spring.
Growth rate: Fast.
Soil needs: Neutral or slightly acid; good drainage required.
Treatment: Cut back any encroaching stems after flowering.
Propagation: By summer cuttings, or by layering in spring.

containers, when watering and feeding can take place at the same time. Liquid feeding can also be done with a diluter, or a hand-held device fixed to the end of a hose. It is important to ensure that no back-syphoning occurs when the diluter is linked to the public water mains. It is, in fact, illegal to attach such a device directly to the mains without suitable equipment.

Correct timing of fertilizer application is important to avoid waste. A dormant plant is unable to make use of fertilizer and so any applied during winter is likely to be wasted. Spring is a good time to feed the plants, with another application during summer. Much later than the end of summer will be wasteful and could encourage soft growth unable to withstand the low temperatures to follow in winter.

Mulching

Incorporation of bulky organic material at the time of planting will boost the soil reserves, but bacteria and other organisms will soon deplete the level. The only way to ensure that the humus content remains satisfactory is to apply a surface mulch.

An annual mulch of rotted manure, garden compost, leaf mould, coir or some other bulky organic material will do much to keep the soil fertile. A depth of 2–3in (50–75mm) should be sufficient to help conserve soil moisture in the summer and suppress annual weed growth at the same time. The mulch may need to be replenished again during the year: much depends on factors such as soil acidity or alkalinity, which in itself has a bearing on the activity and types of worms and other organisms present in the soil.

There are other advantages to mulching: it suppresses moss and lichen; keeps roots cooler during hot weather, warmer in cold (in fact, it tends to even out extremes of temperature); it prevents a pan being

Passion fruits stand a better chance of ripening when the plant is given wall protection.

*Honeysuckle (*Lonicera sempervirens*) is decorative and attracts nectar-feeding insects into the garden.*

formed during heavy rain; and it stops soil being splashed onto the leaves. Some mulching materials, like processed bark, are also aesthetically pleasing; pebbles – available in different colours – can give the same effect, but of course, they do not add to the nutrition or humus content of the soil. A comparatively new product, consisting of wood chips baked at high temperature and then 'mineralized' to reduce rotting, is in the same category. The chips are dyed with various colours, including green, redwood, and brown. Light colours may be used to brighten up a shady spot, or colours may be mixed to create a subtle mosaic in the garden to complement the plants.

Extra nitrogen should be applied to the soil when sawdust, wood shavings and other organic materials lacking in plant foods are used as a mulch. Such material should be free from tannin, turpenes and other toxic substances. Polythene sheeting is useful to suppress weed growth and to help conserve soil moisture. However, it can look unsightly unless it is covered by soil and it should not be used to cover badly drained soil otherwise stagnation may result.

Pruning

'Keep it simple' is a good rule to follow when pruning. First establish whether pruning is needed at all by considering the various reasons for cutting into the plant. Pruning is carried out to remove damaged and diseased parts, to remove old and spent growth to make room for new, to prevent congestion or remove congested growth when it has occurred, and to cut out weak, unproductive shoots; pruning is also done to train and shape a plant.

The removal of a lot of growth (hard

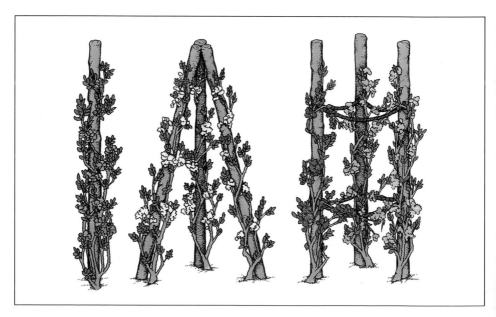

Plant growth can be kept tidy and more restricted by pinching out the tips of side-shoots from time to time, or by tying in the straggly stems.

Future planning is a requirement for successful pruning; here, a well-balanced plant has resulted from thoughtful training.

pruning) in winter usually stimulates vigorous growth during the following growing season; summer pruning often has the opposite effect, thus reducing subsequent vigour. Unfortunately all plants cannot be pruned at the same time in the same way. When a plant is pruned at the wrong time the amount of subsequent blossom is often reduced. The majority of plants, except those grown for fruit production, are usually pruned immediately after the flowers fade. This will give sufficient time for the plant to recover and make way for new, healthy growth which will flower when the proper time comes round again. Pruning can be unpleasant during frosty weather, and the plant is susceptible to bark splitting and disease when pruned under such conditions.

Plants that flower in the winter and spring, or early summer, on growth made the previous year should be cut back after

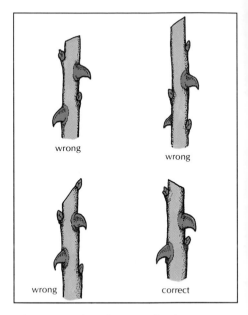

wrong   wrong

wrong   correct

Clean cuts made at the correct height above a growth bud will do much to prevent die-back disease.

Solanum crispum
Hardiness: Slightly tender.
Care rating: Easy.
Description: Evergreen to semi-evergreen, woody-stemmed, scrambling climber.
Peak interest: Summer.
Growth rate: Fast.
Soil needs: Fertile and well-drained.
Treatment: Thin out congested growth in spring.
Propagation: By seed in spring; by semi-ripe cuttings in summer.

flowering to within two to three growth buds of the older framework. Plants that flower on both last year's and the current year's growth in spring and summer should also be pruned after flowers fade. Plants that flower on the current season's growth in summer or autumn should be pruned in late winter after the risk of severe frost has passed. Plants grown primarily for their brightly coloured bark should be cut hard back in spring.

Cuts should be clean without jagged edges, and for this sharp implements are required. A good pair of secateurs is ideal for the job; loppers may be necessary for some subjects like prickly climbing roses and plants with thick, tough stems. Cut the stem cleanly, just above a growth bud. Wound-sealing paints should be avoided because they are inclined to seal disease spores into the cut.

4 • SUPPORTS AND STRUCTURES

Climbing plants have adapted themselves to make use of neighbouring plants or other supports to grow upwards. Some plants like wisteria twine around their support, and around themselves, to give added strength. Twining plants have long internodes between their leaf joints and need to be kept well trained otherwise they soon look untidy and out of hand. Sometimes it is necessary to attach a stray stem to its support, but take care – some plants twist their stems clockwise, while others go anticlockwise.

need further help of one kind or another. One way of doing this is to use special nails with a strip of soft metal attached, which are designed especially for this purpose. The nail is driven into the wall and the metal strip is then folded around the stem.

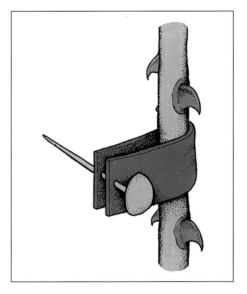

Stems can be fixed to a wall or fence by special nails with a lead strip attached; a strip of leather or plastic serves the purpose just as well.

A pergola can be constructed from stout poles or from sawn timber; it makes an excellent support for climbing plants; especially an outdoor grape vine.

Certain plants like the sweet pea modify some of their leaves into sensitive tendrils. In the case of clematis, it is the leaf stalk which is sensitive to contact. The ivy and 'climbing' hydrangea cling to a surface by producing small adventitious roots from the shaded side of the stem. Once the roots are dislodged from their support, new roots need to be produced before the plant is able to attach itself to the new support.

Plants like the ivy require no more than a vertical surface to cling to, but other kinds

Very old dwelling houses and garden walls often have many small holes resulting from the use of such nails. Some caution is necessary when employing this kind of support because in stormy weather there is the possibility that heavy, wet foliage may pull the supports from the wall. Galvanized wire stretched between bolts or vine-eyes is another way of providing support. The horizontal wires are spaced 6–8in (15–20cm) apart, according to the kind of plant grown.

Plastic-covered wire netting makes a useful and convenient support. Use the plastic-covered type in preference to the ordinary

vines trained along fence and
tied to the rail at intervals

training wire stapled to posts

Self-supporting plants will cling to an open support, such as a solid wall or fence, but the majority of climbers will need extra assistance.

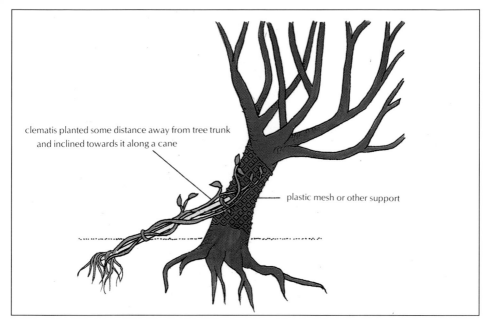

Plastic covered mesh helps to establish climbing plants until they reach the tree branches.

galvanized chicken wire because the latter tends to rust; in any case, the green or brown colour of the plastic kind is visually more attractive. Polythene and plastic netting is a useful aid: one of the main advantages is that it is easily cut with ordinary scissors. Netting is particularly useful for wrapping around vertical posts and for fixing to other awkwardly shaped structures. Trellis is another good method of

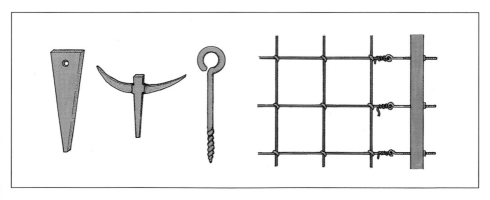

Vine-eyes and wall nails give a professional touch to the job.

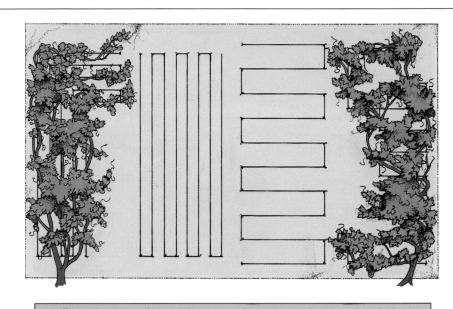

Different designs can be made by training plants to grow along wire stretched between vine-eyes.

Ready-made mesh with large squares is available from agricultural suppliers and other outlets; it saves a lot of time during construction.

support, but the laths should be treated with wood preservative to prevent rotting. Although creosote is often used, it is caustic and so it should be used with care; proprietary wood preservatives are preferable because they are less harmful to plants.

Structures built for climbers and wall plants should be sturdy so that they can support the considerable weight of a mature plant in full leaf. Having said that, there are examples where the plants themselves are holding up an old shed! Certain kinds of vigorous, fast-growing plant like the Russian vine are excellent for camouflaging an unsightly structure. Pergolas, arches, summer houses, gazebos and obelisks can all be decoratively furnished to make interesting features. One simple but effective support can be made by arranging stout bamboo canes in the shape of a wigwam. A similar frame can be constructed from lengths of timber or metal tube. This is ideal for

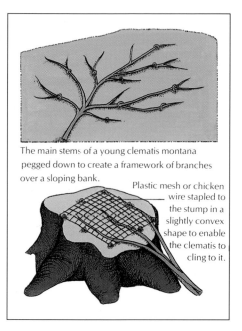

The main stems of a young clematis montana
pegged down to create a framework of branches
over a sloping bank.

Plastic mesh or chicken
wire stapled to
the stump in a
slightly convex
shape to enable
the clematis to
cling to it.

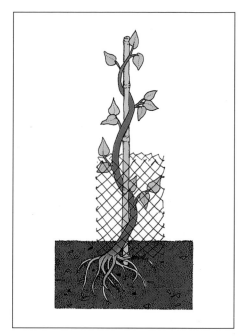

*Climbers need not be growing vertically to
make an attractive feature. A sloping
bank, or the horizontal surface of a lopped
tree, will display the plant to advantage.*

*Special plastic guards are available to
protect plants from animals; alternatively
netting can be used as illustrated.*

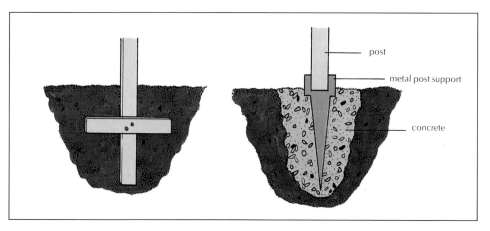

post

metal post support

concrete

*Special metal-post supports are available to give stability and to keep the timber above ground
(preventing rot); alternatively, movement can be prevented by fixing a cross-member to the
upright, but use brass screws because they will not rust.*

A gazebo was often placed at the end of a long path when gardens were larger than the average ones of today. They can still make an attractive retreat during a hot summer evening.

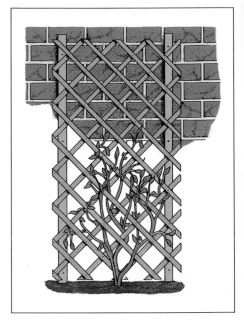

Fixing a wooden trellis to the wall by means of vertical laths of wood allows space between trellis and wall to enable the plant to twine itself right round the support.

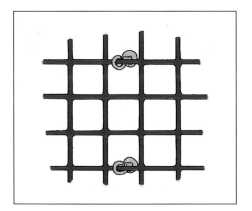

Painting a wall that is clad with plant supports can be tedious, unless hooks have been provided so that the support can be lifted away.

annuals like sweet peas: the plants can be twisted around string stretched from pegs in the ground to the top of the frame.

Where space permits, a very attractive feature can be made from a series of stout posts driven into the ground approximately 15–20ft (4.5–6m) apart; thick rope is attached to the top of the poles so that it falls slightly slack in between. Climbing roses trained up and along this structure look very attractive. Interesting features can be made out of an old tree by planting a climbing plant alongside it so that it scrambles up between the branches. Plants with limited seasonal interest can be made to look more attractive by providing them with a companion: a good example of this is to plant a clematis close to holly.

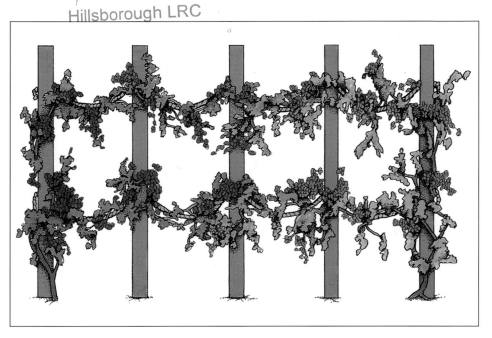

Climbing roses or other plants trained along a rope hung between posts make a very attractive feature.

Patios and courtyards can be made more attractive by growing plants in containers; here, a summer house has also been constructed on the hard surface.

Ipomoea violacea Morning Glory
Hardiness: Tender.
Care rating: Easy.
Description: Vigorous twiner with soft stems.
Peak interest: Summer.
Growth rate: Fast.
Soil needs: Poor, or fertile and well-drained.
Treatment: Deadhead faded flowers.
Propagation: By seed.

5 • PROPAGATION

Raising plants can be a fascinating occupation and can give a great sense of satisfaction. Plants may be required, for example, to furnish a new project like a pergola, fence or wall, or to give to friends. Whatever the reason, climbers and wall plants can be propagated by various methods; these include seed, cuttings, layering, suckers and grafting.

Hibiscus syriacus *'Caeruleus Plenus'* *produces its flowers over a long period.*

There is usually a preferred method of propagation for each different kind of plant, although it is always interesting to experiment with various methods to see which works best for you. 'Green-fingered' gardeners appear to be able to encourage roots to grow on the most difficult subjects but success really amounts to providing the correct environment for propagation: temperature, moisture, relative humidity, oxygen, and for leafy plants, carbon dioxide and light must be provided at the correct intensity and duration. The rooting or sowing medium must be free from pests, diseases, toxins and excessive amounts of fertilizer. It is also important to propagate from pest- and disease-free stock, otherwise

the parasite is most likely to be increased at the same time.

Seed

Several climbers and wall plants set viable seed so that home-saved seed can be a good source of new plants. However, hybrids or closely related plants which have been cross pollinated are likely to give rise to seedlings that differ in some way from the parent. This can be beneficial in that the offspring is sometimes superior but it is usually necessary to raise many new hybrid plants in order to find one that is worth growing on. The problem does not occur with 'straight' cultivars. Purchased seed is relatively inexpensive and many plants can be raised at the same time. While the seed from some plants germinates quickly, other kinds can take a year or more to appear. In all cases, it usually takes much longer for a plant grown from seed to reach maturity, compared with one grown from a cutting or some other vegetative means.

Certain kinds of seed, especially those

Crinodendron hookeranum *is sometimes listed in catalogues as* Tricuspidaria lanceolata.

surrounded by a fleshy pulp, are best stratified. This involves storing them in cool, moist conditions in the presence of air. One method is to place the seed in alternate layers with sharp sand, or peat and sand mixture in pots or boxes which are buried 6in (15cm) deep in well-drained soil. The contents of the container will then undergo low temperatures during winter. A period of stratification from between two to eighteen months may be necessary according to species.

Seeds with a hard seed coat sometimes need coaxing by soaking them in water overnight, preferably in a warm place. Alternatively, the seed coat may be carefully chipped with a sharp blade; treating with boiling water, or alternate freezing and thawing, sometimes works well.

Sow seed evenly and well spaced out on the surface. Very small seed is best sown by putting the seeds in a piece of folded stiff paper and gently tapping the edge of it to dispense them.

Sowing

The seed of some species can be sown directly in open ground out of doors provided the soil is well drained. However, most seed is best sown in containers. Small flowerpots or pans – or, when a large number of seeds need to be sown, seed trays – serve the purpose. A useful method is to use half-pots of the kind dwarf chrysanthemums are grown in. The type of growing medium used should suit the type of plant being grown: bear in mind that some plants require an acid medium, whereas others need an alkaline kind; most subjects require a medium slightly acid – near neutral – for best results. Loam-based medium, particularly John Innes compost, has traditionally been used for most subjects. It consists of a mixture of sterilized loam, peat, sand, lime and fertilizer. The difficulty in obtaining suitable loam has led to the use of various loamless mixtures. These range from sphagnum peat on its own with added fertilizer and lime, to combinations of peat and sand, horticultural vermiculite, coir and processed bark. Ready-mixed proprietary products that utilize these materials are available, and the only additive required to start them off is water.

Measures should be taken from the outset to prevent plant diseases gaining a foot-

Clytostoma violacea is tender and may need winter protection.

hold. This is best achieved by using only clean containers. Fill the container with seed-sowing medium, give the base a sharp tap on a hard surface, and then level the top of the medium with a straight edge. Lightly firm the medium – the base of another flower pot could be used for the purpose – then sow the seed thinly and well spaced out. Fine seed should be simply pressed into the surface, but larger seed is usually covered with the medium to a depth of twice the diameter of the seed. The medium should be moist: when large seed is sown, a watering can fitted with a fine rose is suitable for moistening, although the method used for fine seed is preferred. (This involves placing the container in a vessel of water until moisture can be seen on the surface.)

Cover the container with a sheet of glass to prevent drying out, and then sheets of newspaper to exclude light. The best place for most subjects is a cold frame in the garden, or some other protected area where birds and mice are unlikely to cause problems.

Piptanthus laburnifolius (syn. *P. nepalensis*)
Hardiness: Fairly hardy.
Care rating: Easy.
Description: Deciduous or semi-evergreen wall plant.
Peak interest: Spring-summer.
Growth rate: Medium fast.
Soil needs: Well-drained and fertile.
Treatment: Thin out congested growth in spring.
Propagation: By seed.

As soon as the seedlings appear, remove the glass and paper. Young seedlings are susceptible to damage by strong sun and

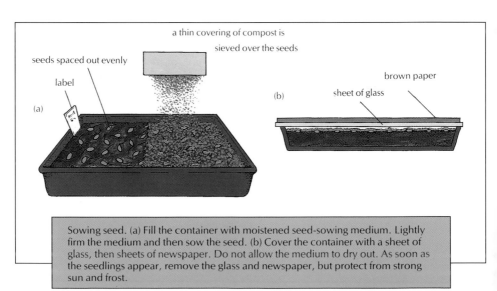

Sowing seed. (a) Fill the container with moistened seed-sowing medium. Lightly firm the medium and then sow the seed. (b) Cover the container with a sheet of glass, then sheets of newspaper. Do not allow the medium to dry out. As soon as the seedlings appear, remove the glass and newspaper, but protect from strong sun and frost.

Prick out seedlings as soon as they can be handled; small plants yet to produce their first true leaf establish much more quickly than larger seedlings. It is important to hold them by their seed leaves rather than by the stem or true leaves as the latter will bruise easily.

frost and so precautions should be taken to prevent loss. When large enough to handle, prick out the seedlings into containers filled with John Innes compost, or loamless medium.

An alternative to raising plants from seed is to increase them by vegetative methods. In this way the new plant can be relied upon to be true to type. However, there are some disadvantages in that there is a possibility of spreading pests and diseases that may be present on the host plant; virus diseases are particularly difficult to eradicate and the necessary equipment is really beyond the scope of the domestic gardener. Seed also has the advantage that it is more easily stored and, while some plant material can be stored for short periods, leafy cuttings in general are more difficult to store and transport than seeds.

Suckers

Stems growing up from the roots below ground sometimes provide the opportunity to make a new plant. Division in this way can be carried out during the dormant season when the soil is not too wet or frozen. The method is to dig up the plant and then separate the roots, ensuring that each portion contains stems and root intact. On occasion, the sucker complete with its root can be removed from the parent without lifting the complete plant. The severed portions are then replanted separately.

Layering

Non-suckering plants, and those that are difficult to root by other means, may be

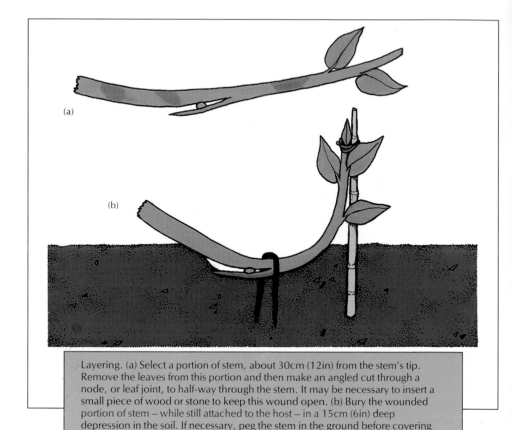

Layering. (a) Select a portion of stem, about 30cm (12in) from the stem's tip. Remove the leaves from this portion and then make an angled cut through a node, or leaf joint, to half-way through the stem. It may be necessary to insert a small piece of wood or stone to keep this wound open. (b) Bury the wounded portion of stem – while still attached to the host – in a 15cm (6in) deep depression in the soil. If necessary, peg the stem in the ground before covering with soil. Firm the soil lightly around the stem. Tie the apex end of the stem to an upright cane, and water in.

layered. This process involves wounding the stem, either by removing a strip of rind or by cutting into the stem with a sharp knife. The wounded portion of stem is then buried while still attached to the host; the apex end of the stem protruding from the ground is tied to a cane vertically. Roots will eventually grow from the wound and, after approximately one year, the rooted portion can be cut from the host and then replanted.

Cuttings

The majority of climbers and wall plants can be successfully propagated from cuttings, although this method can present a challenge because there are variables, like the time of year and the type of cutting, which will determine whether the plant roots successfully. There are three types of cutting: soft, which are taken from new stems; semi-hardwood, which are stems with a firm base, produced during the current growing season; and hardwood, which consist of a firm stem throughout.

Soft cuttings

Soft cuttings are taken from lateral shoots and are approximately 3–5in (75–125mm) in length. To take a soft cutting, sever it from the host, then cut across just below a node. Remove the lower leaves, leaving those that are half-way up and above to function as usual. Dip the base of the cutting into hormone rooting powder and then insert it into the rooting medium. A propagator with misting unit and soil-warming cable is the ideal, although many cuttings will root well when the container is placed in a polythene bag to form a tent. When growth is taking place, roots can often be seen protruding through the drainage holes of the container.

Once they have rooted, pot them off singly into individual containers, or harden them off in a cold frame before planting in the open later.

Semi-Hardwood Cuttings

Semi-hardwood cuttings are prepared in much the same way as soft cuttings, except that they are taken during summer when the base of the stem has slightly matured and become firm. One method that has been used in the past for subjects that are difficult to root is to carefully tear the lateral shoot forming the cutting from its host. This results in removing a small portion of the parent's stem in the form of a 'heel'; the

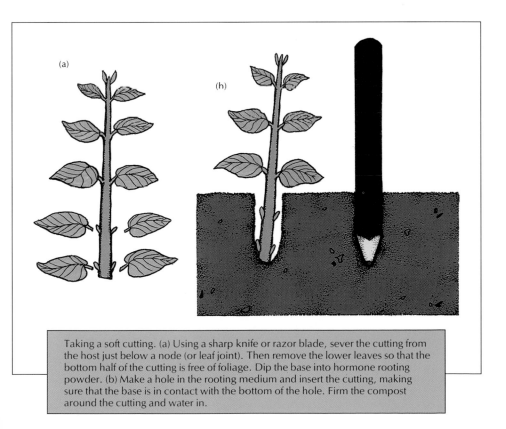

Taking a soft cutting. (a) Using a sharp knife or razor blade, sever the cutting from the host just below a node (or leaf joint). Then remove the lower leaves so that the bottom half of the cutting is free of foliage. Dip the base into hormone rooting powder. (b) Make a hole in the rooting medium and insert the cutting, making sure that the base is in contact with the bottom of the hole. Firm the compost around the cutting and water in.

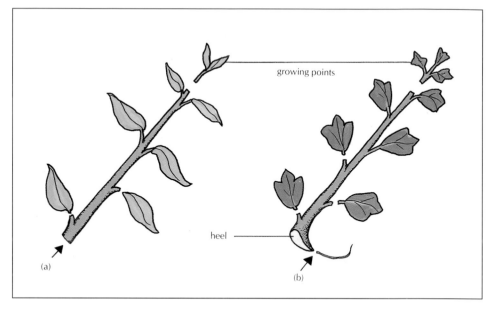

Semi-hardwood cuttings. Remove the lower leaves and the growing point. Cut the lower end of a nodal cutting (a) just below a leaf joint. With a heel cutting (b), neaten off stringy bits of bark attached to the heel.

heel is then shortened to approximately ¼in (6mm) long and inserted in the same way as a soft cutting.

Hardwood Cuttings

Hardwood cuttings are made from the current season's wood that has matured. Late autumn or early winter is usually a good time to take the cuttings. Depending on the species they can be 6–12in (15–30cm) long after removing any immature stem at the top; the cut at the top should be back to just above a growth bud, and below a node at the base. Use a hormone powder suitable for hardwood cuttings, then insert the cuttings to at least half their depth in well-drained soil outside, or in containers in a cold frame. Both evergreen and deciduous plants can be propagated in this same way although evergreens are normally rather shorter and need protection from drying, cold winds.

Grafting

Some plants are difficult to root from cuttings: they either take too long, or do not breed true from seed. These problems can be overcome by grafting a small portion of one plant (the scion) on to a rootstock of another of the same species. For example, roses are grafted, usually by taking a growth bud, together with a small shield-shaped section of outer stem, and placing it behind the rind of a rootstock stem. This form of grafting is known as 'budding'. Another form of grafting involves taking a small portion of woody stem, as if preparing a hardwood cutting, and placing that on a rootstock plant.

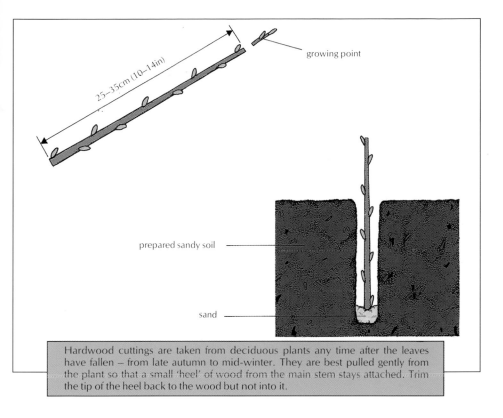

growing point

25–35cm (10–14in)

prepared sandy soil

sand

Hardwood cuttings are taken from deciduous plants any time after the leaves have fallen – from late autumn to mid-winter. They are best pulled gently from the plant so that a small 'heel' of wood from the main stem stays attached. Trim the tip of the heel back to the wood but not into it.

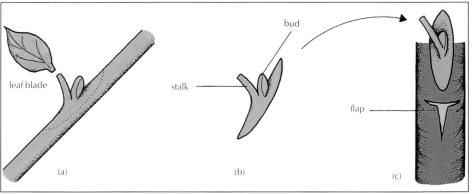

leaf blade

bud

stalk

flap

(a)　　　　　(b)　　　　　(c)

Budding. (a) Select a good growth bud and remove leaf blade. With a sharp knife, remove the bud from its host, together with a shield-shaped portion of outer-stem. (b) To prepare the rootstock, make a T-shaped cut as close as possible to the ground, and then carefully lift the flaps formed by the base of the 'T'. Hold the bud by the leaf stalk and gently push the shield-shaped section down behind the flaps of the cut in the rootstock. The bud can then be secured by winding a length of raffia round the rootstock stem to keep the flaps firmly closed (although it is important not to cover the bud when doing this).

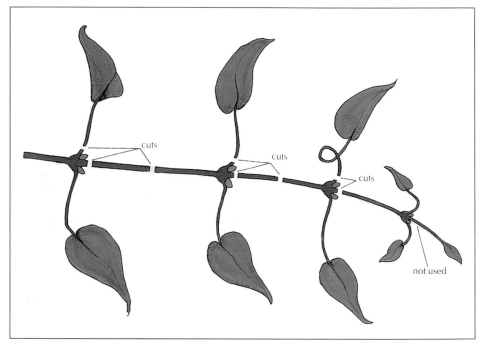

The majority of plants root more readily by cutting the base just below a leaf joint; some vines, however, are encouraged to root faster by making them into inter-nodal cuttings.

Clematis armandii 'Apple Blossom' clambering through a holly tree makes an interesting feature.

The rootstock and scion need to be compatible; the scion must be the right way up when it is placed on the stock, and the cambium (cellular tissue) layers must be close and secure.

It is interesting to experiment with different methods of propagation, especially when successful attempts can be repeated. The best way to ensure this is to keep a diary of dates, and record the kind of rooting medium used, the type of cutting, temperature and other relevant factors (including the name of the plant), so that if it is successful you can repeat the method in the future.

6 • PESTS AND AILMENTS

Climbing plants growing under congenial conditions usually remain healthy for many years. However, they are sometimes prone to disorders of one kind or another, especially if they are subjected to stress. Lack of feeding and dryness at the root during the active season of growth is one way to cause stress; an early warm spell in spring, followed by a cold snap may also cause problems. The majority of plants, then, keep healthy throughout their life-span but in keeping with other living organisms, they may be attacked by parasites from time to time, so it is advisable to be aware of the symptoms if they do occur. Sometimes these symptoms are masked so that diagnosis is not straightforward; for example, drooping leaves may be caused by dryness at the root, but may also be symptomatic of root disease.

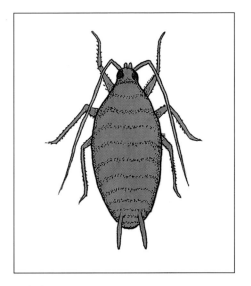

Aphid.

Pests

Ants

Ants make underground nests and disturb the roots, and they swarm over plants searching for aphids to 'milk' for their honeydew. Ants also take certain aphid species below ground and encourage root infestation.

Ants can be caught in jars filled with sweet liquid, such as sugar water; alternatively, they can be discouraged by placing narrow grease-bands around the stems of plants, but this method is somewhat unreliable, especially the case of multi-stem climbers, as the ants could bypass the bands by climbing up the plant supports. Pouring boiling water over the entrance to the nest has proved effective, but care should be taken to avoid damaging the plant's roots.

Aphids

Aphids (also known as *Aphis*, greenfly or plant lice) suck sap and cause distorted leaves and shoots. These pests are often responsible for spreading virus diseases from plant to plant. The honeydew secreted by aphids attracts sooty mould, which in itself is harmless but looks unsightly. Aphids can be removed from the plant by using a forceful spray of clear water, or the colony may be rubbed off with the finger. If it is necessary to use a pesticide, select one that is specific to aphids only so that beneficial insects like ladybirds remain unharmed.

Caterpillars

Caterpillars of various sizes and colour graze on the leaves from time to time. Certain kinds, like the leaf-rolling saw-fly larva which attacks climbing roses, spend their lives protected by a rolled-up leaf. Some gardeners may be happy for their plants to play host; other people look upon these visitors as pests. The larvae are easily dealt with by picking off the affected leaves by hand. When many leaves are affected, the problem may need to be solved by using an insecticide.

Chafer Beetle

Chafer beetles of one kind or another attack plants. The cockchafer, often known as the May-bug, lays its eggs in the soil giving rise to thick, fleshy and dirty-white larvae. The garden-chafer is similar in shape but smaller than the cockchafer. The adults of both kinds eat holes in leaves; their larvae attack roots, which can check the growth of plants, and also cause wounds that allow diseases to enter. The third chafer to look out for is the rosechafer. This is larger than the garden-chafer and has a metallic, bright golden-green colour. Again, the larvae feed on roots. The best way to trap the larvae is to place upturned turves around plants so that the pest can be collected up when they congregate below. Naphthalene is distasteful to the grubs and is often effective when watered into the soil in late spring or autumn.

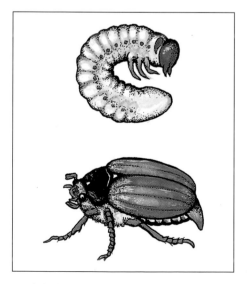

Cockchafer beetle and larva.

Cuckoo-Spit Insect

Cuckoo-spit insect derives its common name from the frothy bubbles secreted by the larvae of the frog-hopper. The larvae suck sap and cause the leaves and tender shoots to wilt and become deformed. The larvae can be removed by hand or, better still, they can be forcibly washed off with a strong jet of water to remove the 'spittle' and insect.

Leafhoppers

Leafhoppers lay eggs below the skin of leaves and the resulting larvae suck sap causing mottling and premature leaf fall. Control is difficult, other than using an insecticide which should be sprayed underneath the leaves and over the ground below to catch those that have hopped off.

Leaf-miners

Leaf-miners tunnel between the upper and lower leaf surface feeding on the contents and causing mines. They are the larvae of small moths and flies. The pest can be squashed between finger and thumb nail, but in the case of a large infestation, it may be necessary to resort to an insecticide. The larvae pupate in the soil below target plants and so it is advisable to spray over the soil surface at the same time.

Mealy Bugs

Mealy bugs are closely related to scale insects; they differ in that the adults are mobile and they are covered by a white, waxy excretion. The colonies feed on sap by puncturing the rind, which often results in the entry of disease spores. A forceful application of clear water is sometimes an effective control; methylated spirit can be used; otherwise it is a case of using an insecticide.

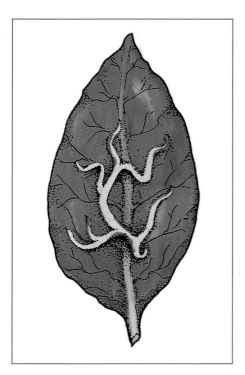

Leaf miner damage.

Scale Insects

Scale insects resemble miniature tortoises, they are approximately ¼in (6mm) in diameter, or less according to the species; others are shaped like a small mussel shell – hence their common name of mussel scale. They are mobile only in the juvenile stage, but at all stages they reduce the vigour of the plant by sucking its sap. The pests secrete honeydew in the same way as aphids and, in this way, attract ants and wasps; the latter inadvertently collect mobile young to deposit on other plants. Inspect any new plant acquisitions carefully for these pests; once established, they can multiply into large colonies very quickly. They can be removed from the plant by scraping them away with a finger nail, or a seed label. Methylated spirit on the end of an artist's brush can also be effective when the insect has lifted its shell to reproduce in spring.

Slugs and Snails

Slugs and snails are among the best known

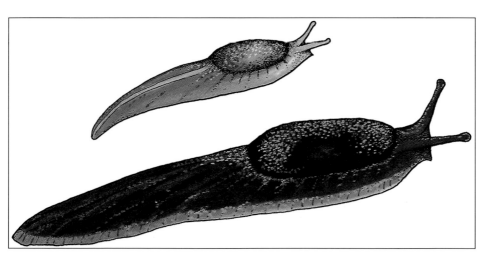

Slugs are a real problem for all gardeners.

Weevil adult and larva.

invaders of plants. They attack seedlings by chewing leaves, and they also eat soft stems. The pests are most likely to come out at night when the air is moist and cool; they can easily be seen with the aid of a torch and dealt with accordingly. Upturned grapefruit skins make useful traps, shallow containers filled with stale beer are also effective.

Weevils

Weevil adults are particularly active during late spring and summer, when they chew holes in leaves. They are difficult to catch by hand because they easily detect movement and then fall to the ground and hide away. Traps made from rolled corrugated paper, sacking, or a piece of board placed below the shrub will attract the pest.

Diseases and Other Problems

Bud Drop

Bud drop can result from birds' pecking at them, especially in spring when the buds are beginning to swell and break open. The usual methods to detract birds are rather unsightly and the shrub border is hardly the place for them. These include silver paper, or other reflective material like a mirror suspended from the plant. Cotton threaded through the plant is sometimes effective.

Repellents in the form of sprays are unlikely to be effective unless they have a gritty texture to make the bud unpleasant for the bird.

Bud drop can also be caused by a lack of moisture at the roots, especially during the short period before bud break.

Canker

Canker disease attacks the stem and produces a sunken lesion, usually surrounded by flaking and corky rind. The problem often arises when two branches have rubbed together, or when a snag has been left at pruning time. To prevent canker, prevent damage to the bark whenever possible; and avoid painting over wounds, but do make them smooth with a sharp blade or rasp. When canker is present, it should be cut out, preferably by removing the branch back to an area where there is no longer any internal staining.

Chlorosis

Chlorosis usually occurs when the plant is deficient in a certain plant food. Yellow leaves at the base of the plant, particularly when the veins remain green, suggests that it is lacking magnesium, possibly as a result of growing in chalky soil. The alkalinity in chalky soil tends to isolate the element so that it is made unavailable. Magnesium sulphate (Epsom salt) is the answer here. Yellow leaves and stunted growth can also result from a lack of nitrogen. Yellow leaves at the apex of the stems is more likely to indicate a deficiency of iron or manganese. In all cases, fertilizers should be applied according to the instructions on the container label.

Coral Spot

Coral spot is a disease that can infect living tissue as well as dead. It produces pinkish pustules and is readily seen. The best way to prevent an attack is to avoid leaving snags when pruning, and to collect up all prunings and other woody material that may be lying about the garden.

Damping-Off Disease

Damping-off disease is caused by a water-borne parasite whose spores are carried in the air from one water surface to another. The disease affects seedlings, causing them to topple over at soil level. The majority of the parasites are introduced by watering from containers where the water has been stored without a cover, allowing spores to be blown on to the water's surface. Infection can also come from using dirty pots and seed trays, and by reusing sowing or potting medium that has been contaminated.

Dieback

Dieback problems can be caused by true parasitic diseases, or they can be physiological or mechanical. Shoots that have died back from the tip should be cut back to just above a healthy growth bud without leaving a snag; avoid painting the wound. If the problem occurs most years, try transplanting to a more favourable position sheltered from frost.

Leaf-Spot

Leaf-spot occurs as a result of attack by a number of different diseases. Each spot is caused by a single spore alighting on the leaf and then sending out minute feeding tubes. The majority of leaf spots appear during damp weather and the best preventive measure is to ensure that there is good air circulation through the plant by correct pruning.

The problem can also be caused by polluted air; incorrect application of pesticide can give rise to leaf spots, as can acid rain.

Mildew

Mildew can be seen as a whitish covering on leaves, stems and buds; in fact all parts of the plant above ground can be affected. Some kinds of mildew produce a brownish covering similar to velvet. These symptoms should not be confused with the natural characteristics of some plants which produce similar features. Plants infected by mildew lack vigour, and their leaves are often distorted and fall prematurely. The best way to prevent mildew is to avoid any check to growth: correct feeding, watering and general care all play a part. While minor infections can be pruned out, the only way to control an advanced attack is to resort to using a fungicide.

Downy mildew often follows after a check to growth.

Rust

Rust symptoms appear as brown or orange pustules. The disease is becoming more widespread in some plants, especially roses. Pruning is sometimes effective but if the problem is cause for greater concern then a fungicide should be used. The parasite lodges in stem crevices and on fallen leaves during winter and so leaves should be collected up when they fall.

Wilt

Wilt causes the leaves to droop and can result from dryness at the root, wind, strong sun after a spell of dull weather, waterlogging, frost thawing too quickly, canker girdling the stem, incorrect use of pesticide, over feeding, or root disease. Of these, the last is likely to create the most difficulty in correcting. One cause of wilt that is extremely difficult to eradicate is honey fungus.

Honey Fungus

Honey fungus, often known as boot-lace fungus (*Armillaria* spp.) attacks a wide range of plants by penetrating the tissue of the roots by means of growths resembling boot-laces. Plants wilt and eventually die because it is difficult to apply a fungicide sufficiently concentrated to eradicate the fungus without seriously affecting the host. However, some people believe that they have saved plants by using phenolic applications and there is at least one proprietary product available with a label recommendation. If a plant is showing symptoms of attack, carefully lift some bark from the stem at ground level. If cotton-like threads of mycelium can be seen below, the chances are that *Armillaria* is present, especially if a honey-like smell can be detected. Sometimes yellow toadstools appear close to infected plants but that is not always the case.

When Honey fungus is confirmed, it would be advisable to remove the plant, together with surrounding soil so that adjacent plants do not become infected. The boot-laces, correctly called rhizomorphs, can travel a considerable distance in the soil to find a new host.

Abelia x grandiflora

A slightly tender evergreen shrub reaching 6ft (1.8m), with white and pink flowers in summer and autumn. Full sun or light shade in any well-drained soil will suit. Pruning is not usually necessary. Propagate by cuttings in late summer.

Abeliophyllum distichum

A deciduous plant reaching 5ft (1.5m). It requires shelter since it produces its fragrant white flowers in winter. Full sun in any well-drained soil is necessary. Prune to remove dead wood and weak growth. Propagate by cuttings in summer.

Abutilon megapotamicum

A semi-evergreen that reaches 6ft (2m) and produces lantern-shaped flowers in spring. The plant is slightly tender and requires a sunny position, although light shade will be tolerated. Any well-drained soil will suit. Thin out old wood in spring. Propagate by sowing seed, or by taking cuttings in spring or summer.

Actinidia kolomikta

The large, purple leaves of this 18ft (5.5m) deciduous plant become variegated as they mature. Full sun or partial shade in any well-drained soil is necessary for best results. Fresh growth should be cut back to

Abelia grandiflora.

within three buds of the old wood in spring. New plants can be raised by seed, or by cuttings during late summer.

Bougainvillaea glabra

A tender evergreen or semi-evergreen plant reaching 15ft (4.5m). It will survive out of doors only in the most sheltered of gardens in the south and south west. It needs full sun and any well-drained soil. The small flowers produced in summer are enclosed in bright petal-like bracts. Prune to keep within bounds. Propagate by cuttings in summer.

Bougainvillaea glabra.

Ceanothus thyrsiflorus Californian Lilac
An evergreen reaching 20ft (6m). It has glossy green leaves and pale-blue flowers that are produced in spring on stems made the previous year. Full sun is necessary for good growth, and well-drained soil is satisfactory. Thin out old, congested growth when flowers fade. Summer is the best time to take cuttings.

Chaenomeles speciosa (syn. C. lagenaria) Flowering Quince
This deciduous plant reaches 6ft (2m) and produces showy blossom in spring, followed by fruit in autumn. Any well-drained soil in sun or partial shade will suit. Prune during late summer by cutting back the current season's growth to five leaves. Propagate by lifting suckers, by layering, or by seed.

Chaenomeles speciosa.

Chimonanthus praecox Winter Sweet
A deciduous shrub that reaches 10ft (3m) and produces fragrant flowers in winter. It requires good light, so full sun or partial shade is necessary. Plant in any well-drained soil. Stems should be cut back by one third after removing congested growth in spring. Propagate by cuttings in late summer.

Clematis armandii
An evergreen that reaches 20ft (6m) and produces clusters of flowers in spring. Grow in full sun or partial shade in any well-drained soil. Thin out congested growth when flowers fade in early summer. Propagate by cuttings in summer.

Clematis orientalis
With this 15ft (4.5m) plant, attractive yellow flowers in summer are followed by feathery seed-heads in autumn. Prune during late spring by cutting back to within one or two buds of the previous year's growth. Cuttings may be taken in summer.

Clematis rhederiana
Reaching 20ft (6m), this plant produces primrose-yellow, bell-shaped flowers on current season's growth during late summer and autumn. Prune in early spring by cutting back all stems to a bud 6–12in (15–30cm) above the ground. Propagate by summer cuttings or by layering.

Clianthus punicus 'Albus' Parrot's Bill
A slightly tender evergreen or semi-evergreen that reaches 9ft (3m) and produces claw-like flowers in spring and early summer. It requires full sun and any well-drained soil. Shorten encroaching stems after flowering. Propagate by seeds sown in spring or by cuttings in summer.

Clytostoma violacea
A tender, evergreen, 15ft (4.5m) plant that produces attractive flowers in summer. Partial shade and any well-drained soil will suit. Reduce congested growth in spring. Propagate by cuttings in summer.

Crinodendron hookerianum (syn. Tricuspidaria lanceolata)
This evergreen, slightly tender, 10ft (3m) plant is best grown in shade or semi-shade. Lantern-like red flowers are produced in late spring and early summer. It requires acid, fertile and well-drained soil. Thin out

Clematis orientalis.

Clianthus punicus.

congested growth after flowering. Propagate by cuttings in summer.

Eccremocarpus scaber Glory Flower

A slightly tender evergreen plant that reaches 15ft (4.5m) and produces bright-red flowers in summer, followed by seed pods in autumn. Any well-drained soil in full sun or light shade will suit. Remove dead branches in spring. Seed sown during early spring, in heat, will produce plants that flower the same year.

Escallonia

This 10ft (3m) evergreen requires a sheltered spot in full sun to do well. It is not fussy about soil provided it is well-drained. Shorten encroaching growth after flowering. Propagate by cuttings during summer.

Garrya elliptica

A hardy, evergreen, 15ft (4.5m) shrub that produces long catkins in winter. Full sun or partial shade and any well-drained soil will produce good results. Thin out congested growth in spring. Propagate by semi-hardwood cuttings in late summer.

Hedera canariensis Variegated Ivy

Evergreen when provided with a sheltered site, the large, variegated leaves make this 25ft (7.5m) plant very attractive. Full sun and well-drained soil give best results. No pruning is necessary, other than keeping growth within bounds. Propagate by cuttings or by layering.

Hedera helix 'Goldheart' Variegated Ivy

Small, evergreen, variegated leaves containing a central yellow blotch are produced by this 15ft (4.5m) plant. Once established, the plant will grow vigorously. Full sun, or partial shade in any well-drained soil will suit. Cut back stems to keep them from encroaching. Propagate by internodal cuttings.

Garrya elliptica.

4 • SUPPORTS AND STRUCTURES

Climbing plants have adapted themselves to make use of neighbouring plants or other supports to grow upwards. Some plants like wisteria twine around their support, and around themselves, to give added strength. Twining plants have long internodes between their leaf joints and need to be kept well trained otherwise they soon look untidy and out of hand. Sometimes it is necessary to attach a stray stem to its support, but take care — some plants twist their stems clockwise, while others go anti-clockwise.

need further help of one kind or another. One way of doing this is to use special nails with a strip of soft metal attached, which are designed especially for this purpose. The nail is driven into the wall and the metal strip is then folded around the stem.

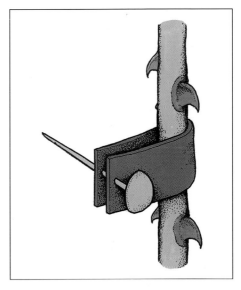

Stems can be fixed to a wall or fence by special nails with a lead strip attached; a strip of leather or plastic serves the purpose just as well.

A pergola can be constructed from stout poles or from sawn timber; it makes an excellent support for climbing plants; especially an outdoor grape vine.

Certain plants like the sweet pea modify some of their leaves into sensitive tendrils. In the case of clematis, it is the leaf stalk which is sensitive to contact. The ivy and 'climbing' hydrangea cling to a surface by producing small adventitious roots from the shaded side of the stem. Once the roots are dislodged from their support, new roots need to be produced before the plant is able to attach itself to the new support.

Plants like the ivy require no more than a vertical surface to cling to, but other kinds

Very old dwelling houses and garden walls often have many small holes resulting from the use of such nails. Some caution is necessary when employing this kind of support because in stormy weather there is the possibility that heavy, wet foliage may pull the supports from the wall. Galvanized wire stretched between bolts or vine-eyes is another way of providing support. The horizontal wires are spaced 6–8in (15–20cm) apart, according to the kind of plant grown.

Plastic-covered wire netting makes a useful and convenient support. Use the plastic-covered type in preference to the ordinary

vines trained along fence and
tied to the rail at intervals

training wire stapled to posts

*Self-supporting plants will cling to an open support, such as a solid wall or fence, but the
majority of climbers will need extra assistance.*

Hibiscus syriacus 'Caeruleus Plenus'

A semi-evergreen shrub reaching 10ft (3m). It requires full sun and well-drained soil with high humus content. Cut back straggly stems in spring; old spent stems may be cut back at the same time. Propagate by cuttings in late spring or summer.

Humulus lupulus 'Aureus' Hop

A vigorous, deciduous, 15ft (4.5m) plant with yellow leaves; flowers are produced on current season's growth during summer. Cut back stems to ground level after leaves fall in autumn. Propagate by division.

Humulus lupulus.

Hydrangea petiolaris (syn. *H. anomala* ssp. petiolaris)

A deciduous plant that reaches 80ft (24m). It requires a sheltered position in full sun or partial shade to do well. Large multi-headed flowers – fertile florets in the centre, surrounded by infertile ones – are produced in summer. Any well-drained soil will give good results. Remove stems growing away from the wall as they appear; dead wood and straggly stems should be cut away in spring. Propagate by cuttings.

Jasminum nudiflorum Winter Jasmine

This slightly tender, partial evergreen reaching 12ft (4m) requires a sheltered spot in full sun or partial shade. Plant in any well-drained soil. The attractive, yellow flowers are produced during winter. Prune in spring to keep within bounds. Propagate by layering, or by cuttings.

Jasminum polyanthum

An evergreen reaching 30ft (9m) with clusters of white, fragrant flowers in late summer and early winter. It is a tender plant which requires shelter and full sun. Any well-drained soil will suit. Thin out congested growth after flowers fade. Propagate by cuttings, or by layering.

Lapageria rosea Chilean Bell-flower

A 15ft (4.5m) evergreen producing waxy, bright flowers in summer. Partial shade and humus-rich, well-drained soil are required for good results. Thin out congested growth in spring. Propagate by seed, or by layering in spring or autumn.

Lapageria rosea.

Parthenocissus henryana.

Parthenocissus quinquefolia.

Lonicera sempervirens Coral Honeysuckle
A tender evergreen or deciduous plant that reaches 12ft (4m) and produces bright, fragrant flowers in summer. Semi-shade and any well-drained soil would suit. Cut out spent, congested growth after flowering. Propagate by seed, or by cuttings in summer or autumn.

Parthenocissus henryana (syn. Vitis henryana)
Partial or full shade will encourage this 40ft (12m) deciduous plant to produce silvery-white and pink variegation in the leaves; they turn brilliant red in autumn. Any well-drained soil would be satisfactory. Prune in late winter or early spring to keep within bounds. Propagate by sowing seeds in spring, or by cuttings or layering.

Parthenocissus quinquefolia (syn. Vitis quinquefolia) Virginia Creeper
A deciduous, hardy plant that reaches 50ft (15m) and produces bright autumn tints. Treat as *P. henryana* (above).

Pyracantha atalantioides Firethorn
Hardiness: Hardy.
Care rating: Easy.
Description: Evergreen, spiny shrub.
Peak interest: Summer through winter.
Growth rate: Medium fast.
Soil needs: Fertile and well-drained.
Treatment: Cut back long shoots to five leaves after flowering.
Propagation: By semi-ripe cuttings in summer.

Passiflora caerulea Passion Flower

A 15ft (4.5m) semi-evergreen that produces flowers of an unusual shape in summer, followed by fruit when the plant is provided with a sunny site in well-drained soil. New growth usually appears from below ground after severe winter frost; otherwise, prune to control congested or encroaching stems. Propagate by sowing seed.

Polygonum baldschuanicum Russian Vine

A very vigorous deciduous plant reaching 40ft (12m) and often used to clamber over unsightly structures. It produces a mass of white flowers in summer. The plant will tolerate full-sun, semi- or full shade and any well-drained soil. It can be cut back hard without detriment. Propagate by cuttings during summer, or by hardwood cuttings in autumn.

Robinia hispida

A 10ft (3m) deciduous shrub producing pea-like flowers in summer. It will tolerate a poor, sandy soil provided it is in full sun. Propagate by seed or suckers in autumn, or by root cuttings in winter.

Tropaeolum peregrinum (syn. *T. canariense)* Canary Creeper

A tender herbaceous plant best grown as an annual in all but mild locations. It reaches 6ft (2m) and produces bright-yellow flowers in summer through autumn. Full sun and any well-drained soil will suit. Propagate by seed or tubers in spring.

Tropaeolum speciosum Flame Creeper, Flame Nasturtium

A 10ft (3m) herbaceous plant producing bright-red flowers in summer. It requires its head to be in full sun, with its roots shaded in well-drained soil. Treat as *T. peregrinum* (above).

Viburnum plicatum 'Pink Beauty'

A deciduous shrub best grown in sun and

Viburnum plicatum.

Tropaeolum speciosum.

Vitis coignetiae.

Wisteria sinensis.

any well-drained soil. It reaches 10ft (3m) and produces white flowers in spring and early summer, which later turn pink; flowers are followed by red, then black, fruits. Thin out any congested growth after flowering. Propagate by summer cuttings.

Vitis coignetiae

A 40ft (12m) deciduous plant producing fruit, followed by bright autumn tints before the leaves fall. Full sun or partial shade and any well-drained soil is required. Prune during winter to keep the plant within bounds. Propagate by seed, or by layering.

Wisteria sinensis

A hardy deciduous plant that reaches 100ft (30m) and produces fragrant flowers in early summer. Full sun and fertile, well-drained soil is desirable. Prune in summer by cutting back current season's shoots to five leaves, then prune to two or three buds in winter. Propagate by seed.

Plants for Special Situations

North and East Walls

Akebia

Chaenomeles
Clematis alpina
Cotoneaster
Hedera
Hydrangea
Parthenocissus
Tropaeolum

South and West Walls

Abelia
Abeliophyllum
Abutilon
Actinidia kolomikta
Ceanothus
Chaenomeles
Chimonanthus
Clematis
Crinodendron
Cytisus
Eccremocarpus
Ipomoea
Jasminum
Lapageria
Passiflora
Robinia
Solanum
Wisteria

Conditions vary from year to year and from garden to garden; even different areas within the same garden can produce variable results from year to year. Since the growth of plants is governed by so many different factors – including site, aspect, soil type, latitude and cultural details like pruning, feeding and irrigation – it is difficult to give precise calendar dates for each operation. One year can be very different from another in the timing of seasons: in some locations, early spring can start off well, only to be followed by a cold spell ending with the possibility of frost during early summer. This means that the detail given in this chapter may well vary when compared with your own particular situation. It can only be a guide and is intended to prompt the memory so that the various jobs can be planned well ahead.

Spring

● The majority of plants will now be showing signs of life, especially those protected by a wall or fence. Shoots showing signs of winter damage, including frost and die-back, plus those broken by the weight of snow or wind, should now be pruned. Early spring-flowering plants will need to be pruned when the flowers have faded. Delay pruning if there is a likelihood of severe frost; in any case, it is better not to prune plants during frosty weather.

● Plants that are not normally pruned but that have already produced flowers that have faded should be deadheaded. Take care not to damage any buds that are just below the spent flower cluster.

● Seeds that have been stratified over winter can now be sown in a nursery bed,

When the roots of a plant are restricted in a container, extra care must be taken with watering and feeding. There are many proprietary plant foods available, all of which should be applied strictly according to the manufacturer's instructions.

or in containers. When the seed is being sown in the ground, it is better to remove any weeds present and then to sow the seed in straight drills to facilitate weeding later on.

● Plant bare-root subjects before the sap begins to rise and leaf buds begin to break. Remember to protect evergreens from cold wind as soon as they are planted. Ensure newly planted shrubs are kept moist at the root, then apply a surface mulch.

● Early blossom that is frosted can sometimes be saved by spraying over it with clear water before the sun reaches it; camellia flowers are particularly vulnerable to early morning sun after frost.

● As the days lengthen and temperatures increase, pests like aphids tend to multiply quickly. Mildew and other diseases that regularly crop up each year may be controlled by a preventive spray of fungicide.

● Now that the soil is beginning to warm up, an application of general fertilizer will help to keep the plants healthy. A surface mulch will also help to keep them happy and do much to suppress the growth of annual weeds at the same time.

Thunbergia alata   Black-eyed Susan
Hardiness: Half hardy.
Care rating: Easy.
Description: Vigorous, soft-stemmed, annual twiner.
Peak interest: Summer, until cut down by frost.
Growth rate: Fast.
Soil needs: Fertile and well-drained.
Treatment: Water freely when growing actively.
Propagation: By seed in spring.

Summer

● The first summer after planting is a demanding time for newly planted specimens, especially those situated alongside a dry wall. It is important to keep the soil moist without allowing it to get too wet. A surface mulch of bulky organic matter or pebbles will help to retain soil moisture.

● The majority of plants that produce bloom on the previous year's growth will have finished flowering by the end of the period and so congested, spent wood should be cut out to make way for new shoots. Others that have started to flower will be encouraged to extend their flowering period if the faded blooms are deadheaded. It is essential to keep spring-flowering kinds moist at the root now to enable them to begin to initiate next year's flower buds.

● Summertime is as good as any for visiting other people's gardens, many of which are open to the general public; the exercise is particularly worth while for getting new ideas. Many of the gardens have unusual plants for sale, which are not otherwise available through commercial outlets.

● Weeds compete with cultivated plants for food, moisture, air and sunlight; they also attract pests and diseases and at this time of year they will need to be kept under control.

● The stems of many plants are at the stage of growth that is ideal for taking cuttings; environmental conditions are conducive to rooting and so early summer is a good time to take soft cuttings; wait until mid- to late summer for those that root more readily from semi-ripe material.

An arched pergola gives good support to climbing plants.

● Late summer is the time to ensure that everything in the garden is prepared for autumn and the change in weather conditions. Supports and stem-ties need to be carefully inspected to make sure they are secure before strong winds damage plants.

Autumn

● Early autumn is the time to plant newly acquired subjects as soon as possible after delivery. If planting is to be delayed, it is essential to prevent the roots of bare-root plants from drying out; the best measure is to heel the plants in by placing the roots in a shallow trench, then covering them with soil. Place the plants at an angle away from the prevailing wind to avoid damage from that quarter. Check availability of fertilizer and bulky organic material so that when the time comes, planting can go ahead without interruption. Frost tends to loosen the soil around the roots of recently planted subjects and so firming may be necessary.

● Hardwood cuttings tend to root more readily when they are taken in autumn, rather than later on. They should be inserted in a sheltered spot in well-drained soil. A sprinkling of grit at the base of the cutting will help to prevent rotting before the roots have formed. The cuttings can often be made from stems that have been pruned.

● Plants vary in their ability to provide autumn leaf colour, which is always an added bonus. Some gardens are still open to the public, and it is worth visiting them to find ideas for suitable subjects; the plants for sale in garden centres and nurseries will also be displaying their autumn tints at this time.

Winter

● The end of the calendar year but not the end of the gardening year for it is a continuous cycle. Choice climbers and other plants continue to thrive in the shelter of a wall. Mature plants with sufficient growth to be taken can provide welcome stems for cutting in mid-winter; these can be taken indoors and forced to bloom out of season. However, a well-planned border can provide decoration at this time without the need to cut and force stems.

● Developing buds may require protection from birds; in rural areas, rabbits can also be a problem at this time. Snow may also cause damage if a heavy fall remains on the branches. Shake snow from the plants so that the weight will not break the stems and cause wounds which would allow the entry of disease spores. The canopy of a high pergola could be reached with the aid of a yard broom.

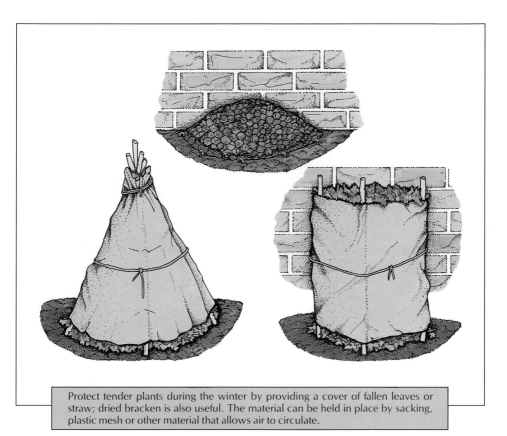

Protect tender plants during the winter by providing a cover of fallen leaves or straw; dried bracken is also useful. The material can be held in place by sacking, plastic mesh or other material that allows air to circulate.

● Planting and transplanting can continue when soil conditions permit. Stems that have been layered, and hardwood cuttings taken a year ago, may be sufficiently rooted to transplant now. Plants delivered from the nursery will possibly be wrapped in straw. This can remain on the plants for a week if necessary, but do take off any polythene that has been attached so that air can move around the plant. Better still, plant the new acquisition as soon as it is delivered.

● Winter is a good time for the construction of new projects, especially if much of the work can be undertaken under cover. However, the turn of the year will see days lengthening, so every opportunity should be taken to catch up on any outstanding work outside.

GLOSSARY

Acid (soil) Having a pH below 7.
Acuminate Having a gradually tapered point.
Acute A leaf with a sharp point.
Adventitious Describes external growth or an organ that is present where it would not normally be; for example, roots growing from a stem.
Alkaline (soil) Having a pH above 7.
Apex The tip of a stem, leaf, or petal.
Axil The angle formed between leafstalk and stem.
Axillary A shoot arising from an axil.

Ball The formation of roots in a container.
Berry A fruit whose seeds are enclosed within a pulpy or juicy substance within a skin.
Bloom The flower. Also a fine powdery, waxy deposit such as is found on grapes or plums.
Bottom heat Artificial heat applied to the base of a propagator.
Bract A leaf-like organ or a degenerate leaf immediately below a flower.

Calcareous (soil) Containing chalk or lime.
Calcifuge A lime-hating plant.
Calciphilous A lime-loving plant.
Coir Processed coconut fibre.
Compost A mixture of loam, sand and cocofibre or other ingredients to make a potting medium for plants. Also, decomposed vegetable material rotted down to incorporate into the soil.
Cultivar Garden variety of plant, or form found in the wild and maintained as a clone in cultivation.
Cutting A portion of root, stem or leaf of a plant used for propagation.

Damping overhead Sprinkling with water to freshen foliage.
Deciduous Describes a plant that loses its leaves each autumn.
Dibber A cylindrical tool, usually made from wood or plastic which is used to make planting holes for seedlings.
Dioecious Describes a species whose male and female flowers are borne on different plants.
Distichous Leaves arranged oppositely, and superimposed in two ranks.

Evergreen Describes a plant that remains green during winter.
Exfoliating Peeling off in thin strips.

Fastigiate Erect growth.
Fertilizer Chemical that provides plant food.
Florets Small, individual flowers within a dense inflorescence.

Grafting Joining one part of a plant to another so that the pieces unite to form one plant.

Habit Manner of growth.
Harden off To acclimatize plants gradually to cooler conditions.
Hardy Describes a plant that can withstand a reasonable amount of frost and low temperatures.
Heeling in Temporarily covering roots with soil until permanent planting can take place.
Hybrid A plant grown from seed resulting from a cross between two distinct species or genera.

Inflorescence The flowering part of the plant.
Internode The portion of stem between two nodes.

Lanceolate Shaped like a lance-head.
Lateral A shoot, stem, bud or root arising from another.
Loam Fertile soil, usually consisting of a mixture of sand, clay and humus.

Monoecious Describes those species

whose male and female flowers are separate, but on the same plant.

Mucronate   The short, stiff point of a leaf.

Mulch   Material, usually bulky organic, placed on the surface of the soil to trap moisture.

Node   The place on the stem, usually swollen, that bears bud or leaf; the 'joint'.

Pan   The surface crust on soil formed after heavy rain. Also a solid layer of mineral below soil level. Also a container used for plant propagation.

Peat   Partially decomposed vegetation, usually acidic, varying in colour from pale yellow to black according to the source.

pH   A scale that measures acidity or alkalinity; pH7 is neutral, below pH7 is acid, above pH7 is alkaline.

Pleach   The training of branches to form a screen or hedge.

Prick out   To transplant seedlings.

Processed bark   Shredded and milled tree bark which has undergone processing by composting to remove harmful agencies like turpenes and tannin.

Propagation   The process of raising a plant. This can be done by sowing seed, by taking a cutting, by grafting, or by division.

Rootstock   The root plus adjoining stem below the union of a grafted plant.

Scion   A portion of plant removed from its host to graft or bud on to another plant.

Semi-evergreen   A plant that is normally evergreen but losing some or all of its leaves during winter.

Shrub   A woody plant that branches from the base with no obvious trunk.

Standard   A trunk without lateral stems below the head.

Stock   The portion of plant consisting of root and stem on to which a portion from another plant (the scion) is budded or grafted.

Stratification   The practice of exposing seeds to frost to enhance germination.

Sucker   A stem produced from below ground level.

Summer pruning   Pruning during the warmest months of the year in order to encourage initiation of blossom buds, and to reduce plant vigour.

Systemic   Describes chemicals that enter the sap stream of a plant.

Tender   A plant susceptible to frost damage.

Tendril   Modified leaf, resembling a whip, that twists around a support.

Topdressing   The application of fertilizer to the surface of the soil.

Trunk   The clear portion of stem below the head.

Variegated   A leaf, stem, or flower with more than one colour.

Water in   To apply water around newly planted roots.

The Sheffield College

Hillsborough LRC

INDEX